Gramtry

When Grammar Meets Poetry

Gayatri Ayn

BookLeaf Publishing

India | USA | UK

Made with ❤ on the BookLeaf Publishing Platform
www.bookleafpub.in
www.bookleafpub.com

Dedication

To anyone who loves to read, especially between the lines!

Preface

Gramtry, a fictitious portmanteau combining grammar and poetry, is what you get when you combine the nuances of grammar and the flow of poetry. Each poem incorporates one figure of speech to convey the message. You can delve into the verses to get a glimpse of how figures of speech are technically applied or to explore how you can harness creativity even from something as mundane and rigid as grammar. You could also go a step ahead and write a poem in response to any or all of them. However, the only condition is to compose the poem utilizing the same figure of speech.

So, get ready to cater to the literary geek in you!
Happy Reading!!

Acknowledgements

A huge shoutout to God for allowing this to manifest and my mother for her genes and the rest.

1. The ALLITERATE A to Z of Life and Love

It is the **a**ccurate **a**mmunition and the **a**cme **a**im.

It is the **b**raced **b**ase and the **b**oisterous **b**rink.

It is the **c**andid **c**ause and the **c**onspicuous **c**onsequence.

It is the **d**efinite **d**irection and the **d**efining **d**estination.

It is the **e**ffortless **e**ffort and the **e**loquent **e**ffect.

It is the **f**irm **f**oundation and the **f**ortified **f**ort.

It is the **g**alvanizing **g**uide and the **g**reatest **g**oal.

It is the **h**eroic **h**erb and the **h**olistic **h**ealing.

It is the **i**ndelible **i**nk and the **i**nfluential **i**nscription.

It is the **j**azzy **j**ewel and the **j**aw-dropping **j**ewelry.

It is the **k**eeper's **k**ey and the **k**ey **k**eeper.

It is the **l**ucid **l**anguage and the **l**iberating **l**esson.

It is the **m**agic **m**antra and the **m**onumental **m**anifestation.

It is the **n**oble **n**ativity and the **n**umbing **n**irvana.

It is the **o**rient **o**re and the **o**pus **o**rnament.

It is the **p**acifying **p**assion and the **p**leasurable **p**urpose.

It is the **q**uizzical **q**uestioner and the **q**uintessential **q**uizmaster.

It is the **r**aging **r**eason and the **r**ewarding **r**esult.

It is the **s**upercalifragilisticexpialidocious **s**eed and the **s**acred **s**anctuary.

It is the **t**rying **t**est and the **t**ried-and-tested **t**estimony.

It is the **u**tilitarian **u**prising and the **u**topian **u**praising.
It is the **v**irtuous **v**alue and the **v**enerable **v**aluable.
It is the **w**himsical **w**ishing **w**ell and the **w**arranted **w**ish.
It is the **x**ylographic **X**ipe and the **x**enial **X**anadu.
It is the **y**ogic **y**ardstick and the **y**awing **y**in-**y**ang.
It is the **z**ealous **Z**en and the **z**appy **z**enith.
It is the A to Z of life.
IT is Love.

2. The Sword and Words
ANTIMETABOLE

Words can be **swords** but **swords** cannot be **words**.
Swords can serve as a **full stop** to bring an **end** but not
every **end** is a permanent **full stop**;
For **nothing** is **permanent** and **permanent** is **nothing**.
But **words** are not **nothing**, although **nothing** is a word.
Words pierce deeper than **swords** and **swords** aren't **deep**
enough to **pierce** the **word**.
Words probe the **soul** allowing the **soul** to **probe** the
foreknown **words**.
Therefore, the **sword** only **changes** the **state of being** but
the **state of being** cannot **change** the **sword**.
Whereas, **words** can **alter minds** and the **mind** can **alter
words**.
A **single word** can **hold** the **world together**; **together**, the
world can **hold** on to a **single word**.
So, **ditch** the **sword** and **pick words** before the **words pick**
on you and the **sword ditches** you.

3. The ANTITHESIS Of Cooking While Fasting

I don't know the reason why but **I'm aware** of this fact unsurpassed,
That I love to **cook** all the more when I'm on a **fast**.
Maybe it's the thrill to see for how **short a while** will my self-control **last**.
Or perhaps it's my **sub-conscious** way to give Ghrelin-resistance a **reality** check at full blast.

I'm unsure about the cause but **I'm certain** of this consequential forecast,
That whenever I'm **low on fuel**, I experience a **high-energy blast**,
To be **innovative** and make even the most **mundane** dish like a connoisseur worthy of broadcast,
Allowing **my loved ones to indulge in delicacies** that ignite **fleeting** memories from the past;
While **I abstain from eating** for a memorable future, with a mind that's **steadfast**.

Therefore, just as we should **feast on occasions**, we should also **fast as a habit** to enjoy beneficial results that last —

To **cross out** the **defects** of our **older version** and to **tick** the **perfections** of our **new cast**.

5

4. Is APOSTROPHE A Myth?

When **God is prayed to**,
He answers through signs and decisions that we have to adhere to.

When **gazing thoughtfully at a tree**,
It chitter-chatters with its rustling leaves gleefully.

When **the sea is approached** with a turmoiled mind,
It roars back in empathy that's rhythmically aligned.

When **a machine is commanded** via a button,
It beeps in acknowledgement but not in high dudgeon.

When the **sky is looked at for inspiration**,
It communicates in cryptic using a cloud formation.

When **memory is summoned**,
It presents audio-visual recordings within a second.

When **expressing to plants** with care,
In return, they respond in kind with the fruits they bear.

When gloomy thoughts **speak to the oblivion**,

It echoes the sounds of the surroundings, bringing one
back to reality's pavilion.

When **fantasizing a conversation** with an estranged
lover,
A reminiscent song resurfaces, substituting for their
claver.

When gratitude is **voiced to the morning**,
The Universe replies a "welcome" via the birds' songs so
warming.

When the **poet addresses the reader**,
The latter is thinking either —
"Meh, whatever" or "Wow! How clever!"

So, when there's a response to every call and uttering,
Is apostrophe still a relevant thing?
Or are we just bad at focusing and listening?

5. Fear No More With CHIASUMS

Never let your **fears** make you **cry**;
for **tears** from **anxiety** make your efforts run dry.

Fear is a **formless notion** while you are **concrete**;
for your **solid** action can waver the **shadowy** entity's cruel greet.

View fear as a deer who is quick to **veer**;
but **gets off the track** when you **look** fear in the eye from anear.

Whenever it **ambles** around, don't **run** away;
chase it, and watch it **ramble** in the opposite way.

Use **fear** like a **fuel**,
to **ignite** your fight mode, instead of the **flight mode**.

For the **birth** of fear may not be in your **hands**;
but how you **handle** it can keep it from **breeding** further and tying you in bands.

6. Literally London, Tropically Tokyo: EUPHEMISMS

"What happened to grandpa?", asked Monu, eagerly
wanting to know.

"He has **given up the ghost**", answered Raman uncle in a
hurry as to the loo is where he yearned to go.

Grandpa was possessed by a ghost? — poor little Monu
misunderstood.

Shocked, he tried to cross check with a woman who
lived in the neighbourhood.

"He has **kicked the bucket**", is all she could manage to
say,

For she had a **bun in the oven** and hence could no longer
stay.

"Monu! Don't trouble auntie. She is **carrying a child**",
yelled his mother.

This elevated Monu's confusion; for the lady was alone
and not holding another.

However, focused on his grandfather, Monu investigated
all the buckets,

Only to find that they weren't kicked about but firmly
stood their ground like tightly shut muckets.

Before Monu could inspect the guest toilet, Raman uncle

dashed into it saying, "I need to sit on **the throne**".

Monu couldn't believe that his uncle was into pretend play despite belonging to the grown up zone.

Then, Monu heard his sister talking on the phone —
"Sorry, Mr. Raman can't talk right now. He's suffering from **Montezuma's Revenge.**"

That's when Monu concluded, "Oh! Uncle is hiding from an enemy. No wonder he looked so blench."

Regardless, he asked his sister about their grandfather once she'd detached the receiver from her face.

To which she replied, "I know it's sad but at least now **he's in a better place.**"

Better place? I can see grandpa lying on his bed but why is he so still?— Monu murmured to himself.

Fed up of everyone, Monu resolved, "I'll ask grandpa myself".

Touched by the longing with which Monu was trying to awaken him from his **eternal sleep**,

His grandfather's soul decided to give him a fractional peep—

"Little one, I'm dead. This body I could no longer keep, but I'm happy so there's no need to weep.

Also, your uncle's stomach is upset, hence he has to frequently excrete".

At last, Monu understood his grandpa's reality, clear and deep.

But now, he was perplexed as to why his family chose to
be so discreet.

7. To HYPERBOLIZE Or Not To HYPERBOLIZE

Ramesh was served his lunch two hours late, yet he didn't **die of starvation.**

Suresh was ghosted for the umpteenth time, yet he was able to **live without her** even in separation.

Kareena didn't make it through NET, yet the **world** didn't **come to an end.**

Tina had a terrible breakup, yet she didn't **vow to never date again** till time's end.

Ajay's mommy didn't believe him, yet he didn't **repeat the truth a million times**.

Ravi's flight got delayed, yet it didn't **take forever** to prime.

Mehu bought a simple gift with his first salary, yet his beloved felt loved **to the moon and back.**

Delnaz felt **on top of the world** when her mother made a healthy version of her favourite snack.

Bhola felt he owned **the best scarf ever** when his dad knitted one for him.

Veena **achieved everything in the world** when her husband kept his word without a whim.

Time seemed to have stopped for David when his bride walked down the aisle.

Seeing the **mountain of books**, Sophia **felt like the richest woman** for the whole while.

13

In short, during a high tide indulge in hyperbole;
When facing a low tide, just let the negative feelings be.

8. Substantial IRONY

The Substance is a movie with a lot of substance about a protagonist who lacks it.
She creates her own substitute to replace her at work as she didn't want to quit.
But little did she know that her identity and fame would be usurped by her own bit.

Initially insecure, she fails to go on a date when she was healthy and fit;
Eventually taking the centre stage, boldly, when she was an ultimate misfit.

In a bid to relive her past, she obliterates her present merit.
She dreamt of controlling her life beyond limit;
Forgetting to give self-control its due credit.

She expected and yearned for the world to see her as legit;
Although to accept her own self she lacked the grit.

She embraced greed, while it was gratitude to which she had to submit.
She thought her substance was without only to realize

that her substance was within and implicit.
She had to lose her substance without to gain her
substance within with full permit.

To feel whole, a fragment of hers she chose to omit,
Unaware that only in uniting her fragments, she could be
a wholesome unit.

To sum it in a line, the film reflects a fact so lit —
The more you run away from something, the more you
ram into it.

Now, did a poem turn into an analytical transcript,
Or an analytical review into a poetic titbit?
I'll leave that conclusion to your wit.

9. Cunning Ms. KENNINGS

Charmed by the aspiration of one day becoming **the first lady**,
Plus, fed up of her **couch potato jack-a-dandy**,
Ms. Kennings was now on a hunt for a man who was a jim-dandy.

In a click, on Crumble, she stumbled upon Sandy,
Who was a **bean-counter** at a company that brewed brandy.
A **tree-hugger**, a **bookworm**, and trendy, he was into everything as refined as organdy.
At least, that's what his profile conveyed which was as loud as a standee.

At a very young age, to **white-death** he had lost his daddy.
Milking this vulnerability, Ms. Kennings soon became his **arm-candy**.
She got his heart to discandy by casting spells via houghmagandy.

They got married but soon after, she wanted to drink his **slaughter-dew** like shandy.
Because he turned out to be a **gas-guzzler** riding, **pencil-**

pusher baddie,
Who was hooked to his **cancer stick** and **postman-chaser**
— Andy,
While also being a **rugrat**'s and an **ankle-biter**'s **baby
daddy**.

Aspiring to someday become **the first lady**,
Our dear heroine found herself a **hot potato** randy!

10. LITOTES And Trends May Not Be Friends

Using litotes **isn't my cup of tea**.
And **neither am I Robert Browning or Christina Rossetti**.

Yet, giving it a shot **shouldn't be a disaster**,
Even though **it may not be a quintessential** spell caster.

Because what I'm about to say is **no rocket science**.
Yet, it's **no mean feat** to bring it to appliance —

That defying a trend may be unpopular but **not necessarily uncool**,
As it **cannot be denied** that blindly following the new school,
Is **no different from** getting entangled in herd mentality's spool,
Which **isn't the smartest thing** to do if **you're not a fool**.

It **won't be a lie** that it's really **not that hard**
To not give a fad an instantaneous white card.
And instead, **not be sorry** to first check,
If the purpose of the trend **isn't a stale cheque**.

Remember, **it's not a crime** to earn the tag of a laggard,

For **it's not as bad as** being labelled a FOMO-driven
haggard.

19

11. Life Is A Birth Chart, METAPHORICALLY

The **Sun is the Father**;
Guiding, energizing, and enlightening us.

The **Moon is the Mother**;
Nurturing, soothing, and nourishing us.

Venus is the Seducer;
Enchanting, entertaining, and satiating us.

Jupiter is the Sage;
Protecting, elevating, and blessing us.

Saturn is the Principal;
Testing, moralizing, and polishing us.

Mars is the Warrior;
Motivating, strengthening, and disciplining us.

Mercury is the Inner Child;
Exploring, expressing to, and negotiating with the world around us.

The **North Node (Rahu) is the Genius**;

Generating, innovating, and pushing new ideas within us.

The South Node (Ketu) is the Stoic;
Levelling, humbling, and chastising the ego in us.

Neptune is the Mesmerizer;
Calming, hypnotizing, and distracting us.

Uranus is the Rebel;
Igniting, liberating, and revolutionizing the id in us.

Pluto is the Ring Master;
Facilitating, forcing, and fortifying change in us.

The Ascendant is the Soul;
Designing, defining, and refining the I in us.

12. Love Through The Lens Of METONYMY

The **pen** is mightier than the **sword**,
But in the matters of the **heart**, keeping **one's word**,
Is greater than the written word.

For **blood** is thicker than **water**, indeed.
But without **water** even **blood** cannot **breathe**.

To merely **bed** the beloved is not love.
Just preparing the inamorato's favourite **dish** isn't love.
Only providing **dough** for the inamorata isn't love.
Neither the impulsive depictions we see **on-screen** is love.
Nor being reported as a couple by **the press** is a proof of love.

Love is **lending a hand** even at the cost of being at a disadvantage.
Love is being the **shoulder to lean on** even when you are in need of a **bandage**.

Love is when two **mortals** understand each other even if they speak a different **tongue**.
Love is to **ear** each other's thoughts even when they are

young.

Love is composing a letter in your own **hand** despite the
digital age.
Love is to **ask for their hand** in marriage in spite of the
hook-up rage.

13. Clocking Time With ONOMATOPOEIA

There was once a time when the phone used to ring **tring tring**.

Now, you either hear the **tralalala of a song** that rings a bell.

But if on vibration, it goes **vrrrr-vrrrr-vrrrr-vrrrr**, sounding unwell.

Earlier, doors had to be knuckle-knocked — **tap tap** or **trat trat**.

Often, you could guess who's visiting by the rhythm, speed, and pressure of the **knock**.

Now, the electric bells either go **ding-dong** or **play an instrumental** like a disc jock.

In the era of hand fans, the wind used to **whisper** with a subtle **fwoosh fwoosh** or **swish swish**.

Now, the motor's relentless **low-bass hummm** is what we hear from an electric fan,

Along with the periodic **tic-tic** or **tak-tak**, if it's as old as a gran.

The alarm clock used to have the universally familiar **trrrrrrrrrring blare**,

Which is now replaced either by a **dhinchak-dhinchak** or **tin-tun tin-tun** bit of music,
Depending on what you find therapeutic.

Spices and herbs were met with the slow and deep **dhup dhup dhup** of the mortar pestle.
Only to be substituted by the **fast, sharp,** and sometime **strenuous growl** of the mixer grinder;
On which research is impending in order to make it **sound kinder**.

Food was associated with the **crick crack crackle** of firewood or coal.
Now, they are displaced by the low-grade and **almost silent humming** of the gas stove,
Or the **somber hmmm** and cartoonish **beep beep beep** of the microwave in the alcove.

Communication was synonymous with **chitter-chatter**, **rustling** of papers, and the **postman's call**.
Now, the **tap tap tap** of the thumbs and **squibbing** delivery notifications have taken over,
Which are subject to transience—vanishing once the fever is over.

Courtship back then was dominated by **uh-huhs, blabber, awws**, and reflective pauses.

Dating now is hijacked by a string of **ooh-aahs, hahas,**
and tatas without any clauses or causes,
Resulting in serious consequences and zero **applauses**.

Utensil **clinking**, babies **goo-goo gaga-ing**, and the
winning team's **hurraying** echoed in homes.
Now, habitats resonate the TV's **banter**, the monotonous
buzzing of gadgets, and silence.
Devoid of conscience, pleasance, and balance.

14. Love: An OXYMORON Only For A Moron

It was a **bright night**,
Illuminated by soft **dim light**.
Done with words, now their **only choice**,
Was to make **silence their voice**.

Intoxicated with love's **open secret** and **surreal truth**,
So **soothingly inciting** and **incitingly soothe**,
They witnessed the **concrete abstraction** of love,
Devoid of **humblebragging** and false pretence's **revealing glove**.

Arming vulnerabilities with **unconscious awareness** for the first and the last time,
Since being **seriously frivolous** with love is a crime,
They explored the **shallow depths** and **deep shallows** of their **embodied souls**.
And henceforth, never felt like **fragmented wholes**.

15. How To Be And Not To Be: The PARADOX

The world is permanently temporary and temporarily permanent.
The side to which you are most resonant,
Will decide whether your turbulences will be tolerable or tolerance be turbulent.

For when you perceive the world to be permanently temporary;
Focusing on the body's mortality, you seek morality in mortal sins.
But when you perceive the word to be temporarily permanent, on the contrary;
Focusing on the soul's immortality, you recognize the freedom in restrictions.

For with discipline, you free your senses from losing their senses—
Indulging in losses that lead to gains.
Whereas, with ultimate liberation, you are bound to the slavery of the senses—
Indulging in gains that yield losses.

With limitations, you are at liberty to let go.

With liberty, you are limited even to grow.

For less is more and more or less,
More lessens—
The innocence, essence and lessons.

So would you still view the world to be permanently
temporary and not temporarily permanent?
Take a pause and let your inner child make this mature
judgement.

16. PERSONIFICATION's Take On Cooking

Cooking is a conspiracy,
Conjured by foods to combat their attention deficiency.

Chopped potatoes, apples, and bananas turn brown;
As if complaining that our negligence lets them down.

Boiling with anger, the tea bubbles, spills, and soils the stove,
As soon as you turn your back on it to fetch some clove.

However, whenever you choose to keep an eye on the tea, real close,
It takes forever to boil, embracing your presence in the corpse pose.

Likewise, when you patiently wait and stare at the veggies to be al dente,
They decide to slow down time, showing you a glimpse of Inferno by Dante.

But God forbid if you opt to leave them for a minute or two.
In fury, they instantly elect to overcook, leaving you

with a mushy stew,
Making you regret the neglect with every chew.
31

Else, if in a nastier mood, the veggies choose to burn out
and stick to the pan like glue,
Forcing you to deal with them anew.

So, you see!
Cooking is indeed a conspiracy—
A phenomenon beyond human coherency.

17. PLEONASM In Philosophy; Philosophy In PLEONASM

Once upon a time, a while ago,
A simple monk was calmly meditating below
A cool, shady, lush green canopy of trees,
When he opened his tightly shut eyes and gazed with pupils that could now seize
A very very deep and unexpected epiphany—

That in this whole wide world and cosmic symphony,
Nothing is a coincidence; there are no coincidences.
For all happenings are divinely ordained celestial incidences.
They occur not a second earlier or later than their set time,
Precisely when all the fragments and segments of God's elaborate detailed plan finally align,
After a long long time.

And it's at moments like these that we better understand the mystery
Of so many unexplained events of our vast and distant past history.

That's why, we are asked not to leave the stage before
the drop of the curtain,
For till the end of the show we must remain for certain.
Or else, we are bound to repeat the same train of torrents
That are inevitably needed to shape God's pattern of
events,
Because destiny is a geometrical design whose curves,
lines, and accent,
We cannot circumvent, prevent, disorient, or uninvent.

And it's through the unravelling of destiny's unseen,
unknown design,
That we grasp and understand how fates of strangers
seem to combine and intertwine.

The monk saw this consciousness unfold itself with his
own third-eye,
Which he conscientiously decided to share with the
whole world before his final and last goodbye.

18. Fun With PUN: The Trial Run

The **Ant** was on a **sting operation**.

The **Bee droned** about it creating a **buzz** without hesitation.

Smelling a rat, the **Cat bristled** in indignation.

The **Dog** tried to **hound** the bee but was soon met with frustration,

Since the **Elephant** had **trumpeted** the dog's intention,

Alerting the bee in time who headed for the stream for protection.

Angered **off the scales**, the **Fallfish** made **schooling** the bee his personal mission.

His friend, the **Goat**, known for its **Capricorn** work ethics, was happy to help him with determination.

The **Hen brooded** over the prospect but **chickened out** fearing a stingy termination.

On the other hand, the **Iguana scaled up** the tree to join the action.

While, **jacked up** on anxiety, the **Jackal feigned** hibernation.

However, the **Kiwi** wasn't affected by the commotion

As its **flight** or fight response **was due for updation**.

The **Lion** lost all his **pride** for he couldn't chase the bee despite the difference in the size's gradation.

Aping the bear, the **Monkeys went bananas**, thanks to
their honey consumption.

The **Nightingale** was a true knight as she **called out for
help**, summoning the entire habitation.

Only the **Ostrich was quick to run for its life** without any
reservation.

Meanwhile, the remaining birds and animals offered
their help without any further persuasion.

The **parrots created a pandemonium** as they mimicked
the queen bee's call to cause a distraction.

The **spirit animal - Quagga - though stripped of its body**,
attempted to **scare** the bee from pursuing its expedition.

Even the **Racoon** quit its **masquerade** party to **claw at** the
bee without due consideration.

Going nuts with the frenzy, the **Squirrels waved a
tailflower** at the bee to obstruct its peregrination.

Taking cues, the **Tarantulas spun a huge web of molten
lava flower** in quick succession.

The **Unau**, a bee sympathizer, **couldn't digest** this and
chose to **turn a blind eye** to the disruption.

By the time the **Vulture** and **his circle** could **scavenge** a
pro-bee proposition,

The **sharp Wasps stung the pests** without any
apprehension.

As hot as the **oven** with anger, **the Xenops** pecked at the
wasps with motivation.

Milking the chaos, the **cold Yak** quietly sneaked out of the farm to end its exploitation.

Knowing the truth **in black and white**, the **Zebra was at a crossroads** and vacillation

About how to tell everyone that the ant was only rehearsing for a film audition.

19. SIMILE's Guide To Losing A One-Sided Lover Like A Pro

He said, "**Like flowers, you add** to my life a sense of pleasance."
So, she became **as toxic as the Devil's Helmet** in his presence.

He professed, "Your **calming** aura is **like** that of **the moon.**"
Thus, she became **as volatile as the celestial body** to get him out of his swoon.

He praised, "Your conversations are **full of depth like a poem.**"
Hence, her chats soon became **as curt and minimal as "M".**

He claimed, "You are **mysterious like a riddle** or a puzzle."
Therefore, she became **as predictable as the clock** as a means to bumfuzzle.

He pronounced, "You **heal like a Goddess.**"
Whereupon, she became **as ferocious as Artemis** with

full prowess.

He remarked, "You **charm like Cleopatra**."
Ergo, for him, she became **as unavailable as her dead body, tomb**, et cetera.

He declared, "Your **company is intoxicating like fine wine**."
In consequence, she became **as sour as vinegar** and **as distasteful as brine**.

He opined, "I admire how you **navigate through life like a river**."
Accordingly, she became **as dark and dense as the Ruki river**.

20. Who Are You?
An Analysis Using SYNECDOCHE

You are not just **another face in the crowd**.
Ask the street dog who views you as a stroud.
For you, he may be just **another mouth to feed,**
But to his snout your whiff is a warming gleed.

You are not just another **corporate hand**.
For, your every caress gives the colony cow a glimpse of
the **promised land**.

You are not a slave to the pleasures of the **flesh**.
The hand that rocked your cradle, sees you as a soul
that's fresh.

You are not just **dust**.
For you are hope for the **hearts** that have put in you their
trust.

Your value is not limited to a **head count** during census,
Or to how much your **plastic** can cover your expenses,
Nor to just an **inked finger** when reaching an electoral
consensus.

For you will always be the friend in deed for that
juicehead buddy
Whose **hand you had held** when his logic was muddy,
And who can now **turn down a glass**, even when life gets
a bit duddy.

You are not just a **cog in the wheel** even if you don't get
the recognition,
For if that were the case, our DNAs and appearances
wouldn't have any differentiation.

21. "It's Fine": The Ultimate UNDERSTATEMENT

Having known each other since childhood and married
for thirty five years,
There were only **a few insignificant things** regarding
Mrs. Rao about which Mr. Rao was unclear.

He could never get it straight that Mrs. Rao was allergic
to peanuts and not pine nuts,
Which **wasn't a biggie**, for each time she would **visit the
loo only five times** to clear her guts.

It was **only 99%** of the times that he got her favourite
dish wrong.
Oh, come on! It's **not as bad as** he mistaking her most
cherished song.
For there was none as she was deaf with both ears gone.

It **wasn't a huge problem** that he got her a blue sapphire
instead of a yellow one.
After all, aren't colours and **gemstones just for fun**?

Diligently every year, he used to wish her on her
birthday,
Barring **the minor error** of getting the month a bit astray.

Regardless, their relationship aged like fine wine,
At least that's how Mr. Rao would summarize it in a line,

Because whenever he committed a **booboo that was far from malign**,
Mrs. Rao would react with a **barely honest—"It's fine."**

22. The Life Path By ZEUGMA

He took the **right measures** to get the perfect fit and to make life an ultimate hit.

He was **bright** and so was his aura which blossomed like a pleasant flora.

He was **high** on morals and never on his laurels.

He **lit** the room with his charm; not substances that cause harm.

He **broke** records but never promises and hearts even during discords.

His clothes, his speech, his manners, and his thoughts were **well-refined.**

His jawline was **well-defined** apart from his principles that could spellbind.

To the beholders, he was a **vision** and so were his life goals and missions.

Embracing self-control, he never **lost** his patience, dignity, and faith in God at any cost.

For he **calibrated** his actions to the depth and also his breath,

Which helped him **conquer** his mind and the hearts of all who had a mind.

This is how he managed to have a **blissful** life and ending.

www.ingramcontent.com/pod-product-compliance
Lightning Source LLC
LaVergne TN
LVHW050943200726
843508LV00011B/2433